E.P.L.

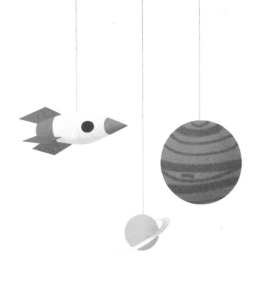

SPACE KIDS

An Introduction for Young Explorers

Illustrated by **ANDREA DE SANTIS**
Written by **STEVE PARKER**

LITTLE
GESTALTEN

EVERYTHING, EVERYWHERE

Look up at the night sky. All you can see is ... me. I am <u>Space</u>. I am everything, everywhere.

SUPERNOVA

GALAXY

STAR

PLANET

Space began as a tiny speck, even smaller than this "o"! Then there was a Big Bang and the tiny speck exploded ... BOOM! It seems unimaginable! But that was the start of everything. That was over 13 billion years ago. Ever since, space keeps growing bigger.

WHERE STARS BEGIN

I am Nebula, a great wispy, misty cloud of gas and dust. I am the parent of stars. In me they are born …

This is the **WITCH HEAD NEBULA**. It glows with a faint blue light.

Many nebulas are named after their shape. This is the **HORSEHEAD NEBULA**. Its clouds stop light passing through to us, so it looks dark.

No one knows how many nebulas there are. There could be trillions … Yet each one has a different size and shape.

SHINING BRIGHT

I look like a tiny dot twinkling in
the darkness but come closer ...
I am a giant ball of burning flames.
I am <u>Star</u>.

WHITE DWARF A medium-sized star with
a pale glow. It is shrinking and fading.

SUPERGIANT The biggest of all stars,
sometimes 1,000 times larger than the Sun!

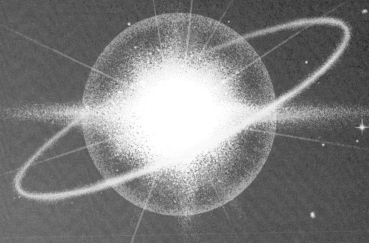

RED DWARF The most common and
coolest star. It is smaller than our own
star, the Sun.

SUPERNOVA A giant star that goes BANG!
One of the biggest explosions in space,
it lasts for weeks or even months.

There are many kinds of stars. Small ones last for trillions of
years. The biggest only live a few million. A star's color shows
how hot it is. Bluish stars are scorching. Reddish ones are 10
times cooler—yet still burning hot!

SHAPES IN THE STARS

I am Constellation, a pattern of stars in the sky. It takes imagination to see me, but I'm here if you look.

LIBRA, the Scales

LEO, the Lion

HERCULES, the Hero

ARIES, the Ram

URSA MINOR, the Little Bear

LUPUS, the Wolf

CANCER, the Crab

CASSIOPEIA, the Queen

Long ago, before electric lights lit our nights, people had plenty of time for stargazing. They looked up in wonder and saw the shapes of animals, people, and gods. Almost 2,000 years ago a Greek stargazer named 48 constellations. Today scientists name 88. Can you see what they see?

GALAXIES

See me running along the sky
like a milky-white line of stars? I'm
your galaxy. My name is <u>Milky Way</u>.

The Milky Way is like a
city in space, each star a
different neighborhood.
Our star is the Sun and
it lives in the Milky Way.
There are about 250 billion
stars in the Milky Way ... so
250 billion neighborhoods.

The **MILKY WAY** is a spiral galaxy, from outside it looks like this.

SMALL MAGELLANIC CLOUD
Irregular galaxies are faint
clouds in any shape.

At the center is a black hole. Anything that comes near falls in and disappears!

VIRGO A
An elliptical galaxy is rounded like an egg.

Because space is getting bigger, all **GALAXIES** are moving away from each other at amazing speed.

9

BRIGHT AND HOT

Ancient Egyptians worshipped me as Ra. Ancient Romans called me Apollo. You can call me <u>Sun</u>.

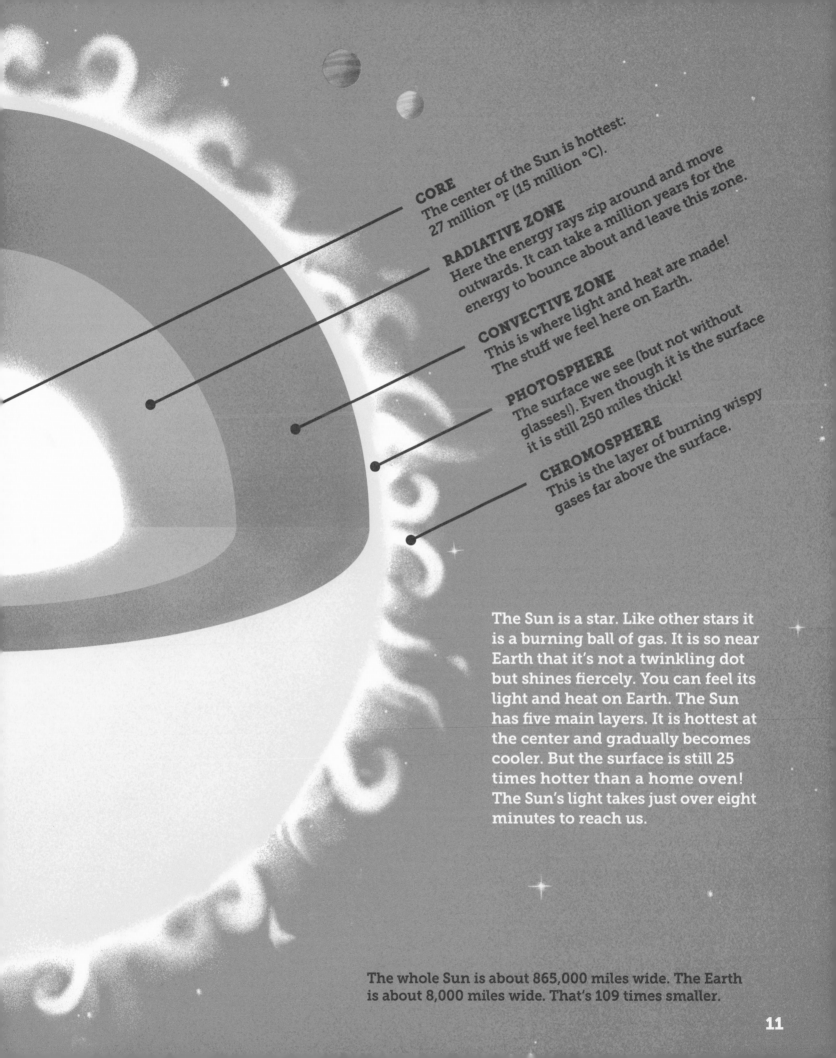

CORE
The center of the Sun is hottest:
27 million °F (15 million °C).

RADIATIVE ZONE
Here the energy rays zip around and move
outwards. It can take a million years for the
energy to bounce about and leave this zone.

CONVECTIVE ZONE
This is where light and heat are made!
The stuff we feel here on Earth.

PHOTOSPHERE
The surface we see (but not without
glasses!). Even though it is the surface
it is still 250 miles thick!

CHROMOSPHERE
This is the layer of burning wispy
gases far above the surface.

The Sun is a star. Like other stars it
is a burning ball of gas. It is so near
Earth that it's not a twinkling dot
but shines fiercely. You can feel its
light and heat on Earth. The Sun
has five main layers. It is hottest at
the center and gradually becomes
cooler. But the surface is still 25
times hotter than a home oven!
The Sun's light takes just over eight
minutes to reach us.

The whole Sun is about 865,000 miles wide. The Earth
is about 8,000 miles wide. That's 109 times smaller.

THE SUN'S FAMILY

I am your Solar System, a huge family in space. My center is the Sun and spinning around me are my eight planets.

MERCURY This rocky planet is the smallest. It is so close to the sun it is burning hot.

JUPITER The biggest planet. Like the other three outer planets, it is not solid but a "gas giant."

URANUS It has rings like Saturn's, but they are very faint.

NEPTUNE Its mix of gases make a blue-green color. Neptune is so far it is freezing!

SATURN The second-largest planet, with many beautiful rings around the middle.

EARTH Our home world has rocks and clouds, and it is the only planet with liquid water!

MARS The fourth rocky planet. The surface has mountains, valleys, and windblown red dust.

VENUS Rocky with hills and valleys, but always covered in thick clouds.

A solar system is one star and everything moving around it, such as planets and moons. They all keep moving around the same paths because of a pulling force called gravity. Everything has gravity. Gravity on Earth keeps the Moon traveling around it. Our Sun has more gravity and so keeps the planets on their paths.

13

SPACE WANDERERS

Most asteroids are between the planets Mars and Jupiter. This is the **ASTEROID BELT**, and there are millions of them inside it.

The biggest **ASTEROIDS** are more than 310 miles across. That's as wide as a country like England. The smallest asteroids are no larger than a school bus.

I am <u>Asteroid</u>, a lumpy chunk of rock whizzing through space. I'm too small to be a planet. But just like planets, I go around the Sun.

I am <u>Comet</u>, the loneliest of space wanderers. When I come near the Sun, its rays make me shine brightly with a long, beautiful tail.

About 66 million years ago, a comet or asteroid smashed into Earth. It set off volcanoes and created floods that wiped out the dinosaurs.

15

3, 2, 1,
BLAST OFF!

No other machine is as powerful, fast, or noisy as me! I am Space Rocket! I am the only way to reach space.

A rocket's engine must be super powerful to blast into space. To escape the pull of Earth's gravity the rocket must reach a speed of 7 miles per second! When a space rocket has finished its mission it might drift away into deep space or fall back to Earth and burn up in a fireball!

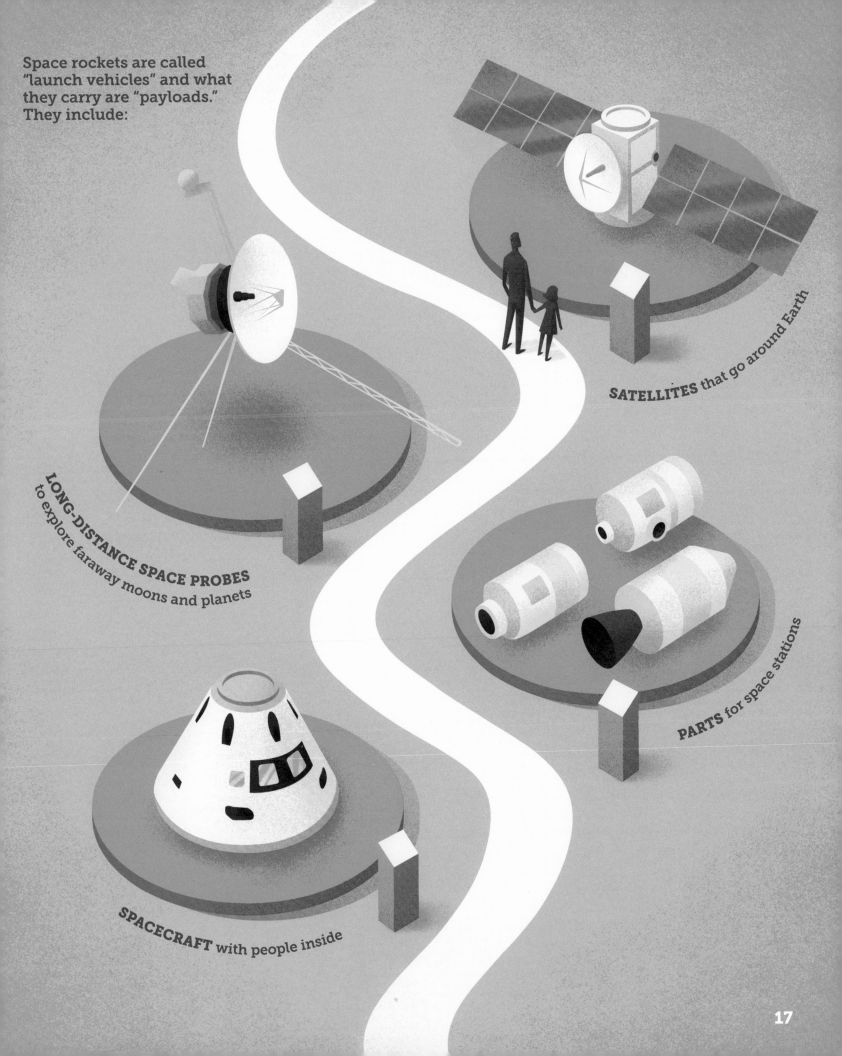

Space rockets are called "launch vehicles" and what they carry are "payloads." They include:

SATELLITES that go around Earth

LONG-DISTANCE SPACE PROBES to explore faraway moons and planets

PARTS for space stations

SPACECRAFT with people inside

17

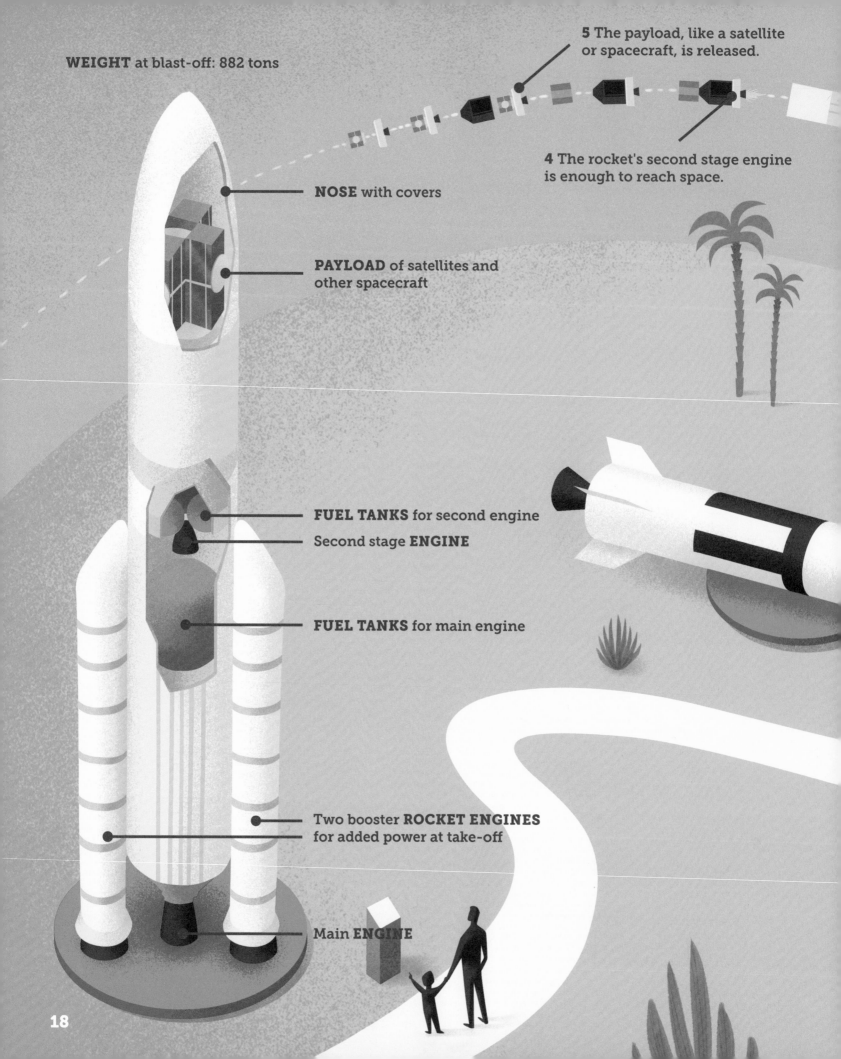

WEIGHT at blast-off: 882 tons

5 The payload, like a satellite or spacecraft, is released.

4 The rocket's second stage engine is enough to reach space.

NOSE with covers

PAYLOAD of satellites and other spacecraft

FUEL TANKS for second engine

Second stage **ENGINE**

FUEL TANKS for main engine

Two booster **ROCKET ENGINES** for added power at take-off

Main **ENGINE**

BUILDING A ROCKET

I am <u>Ariane 5</u>, one of the best rockets in the world. More than 100 like me have been built.

3 After nine minutes the main engine switches off and falls away.

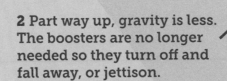

2 Part way up, gravity is less. The boosters are no longer needed so they turn off and fall away, or jettison.

1 Ariane's main engine and two boosters all fire at blast-off for the greatest power against the force of gravity.

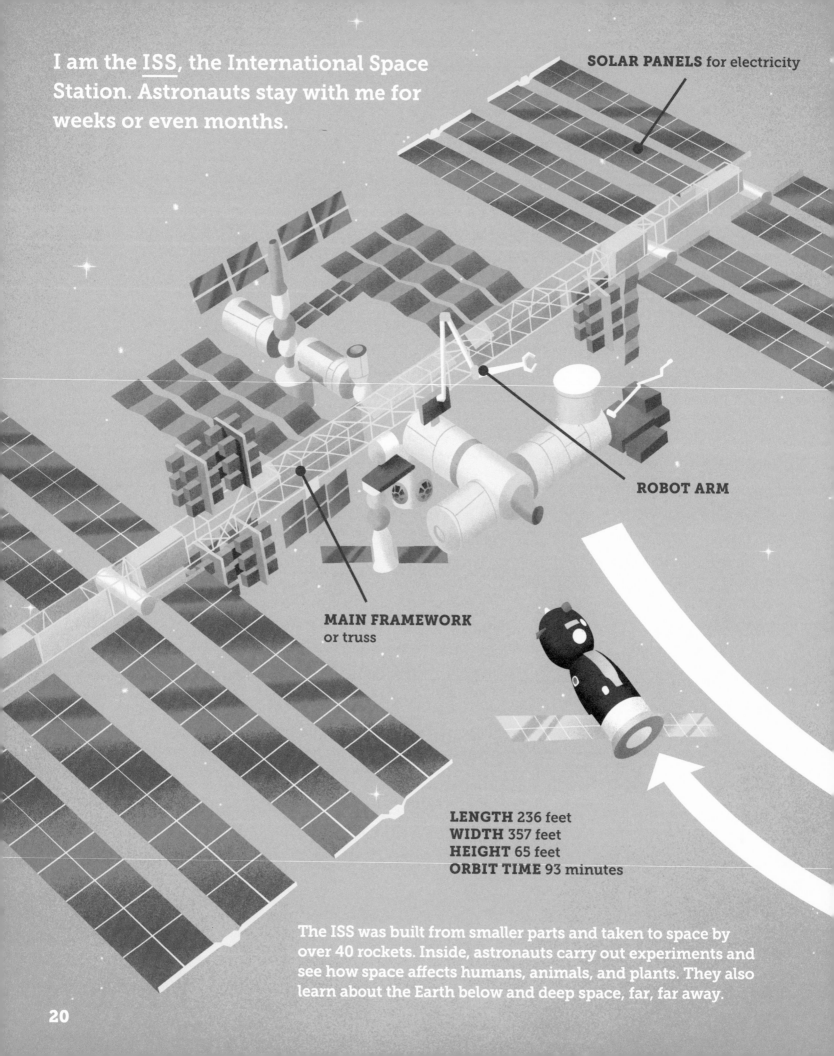

I am the <u>ISS</u>, the International Space Station. Astronauts stay with me for weeks or even months.

SOLAR PANELS for electricity

ROBOT ARM

MAIN FRAMEWORK
or truss

LENGTH 236 feet
WIDTH 357 feet
HEIGHT 65 feet
ORBIT TIME 93 minutes

The ISS was built from smaller parts and taken to space by over 40 rockets. Inside, astronauts carry out experiments and see how space affects humans, animals, and plants. They also learn about the Earth below and deep space, far, far away.

A HOME IN SPACE

Main **LIVING AREA**

Columbus, Destiny, and Kibo
SCIENCE WORKROOMS

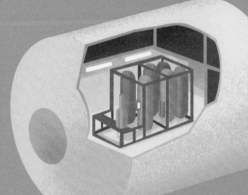

LIFE SUPPORT SECTION
for air and water

STORAGE AREAS

Visiting robot spacecraft with **FOOD AND SUPPLIES**

Visiting Soyuz spacecraft with **NEW ASTRONAUTS**

LET'S GO INTO SPACE

Calling planet Earth! I'm a space traveler, or an **Astronaut** if you like.

CUPOLA has windows for observing Earth and space.

Our **FOOD** is mainly dried. We add water and heat it.

Our **SHAMPOO** is like powder and needs no water.

To become an astronaut you need to learn all about space. You also need to be calm and cool. If something goes wrong in space, YOU must fix it.

We use normal **TOOTHPASTE**, but we swallow the foamy stuff.

We use a normal **TOILET**, but our body waste is quickly sucked away, like a vacuum cleaner.

We sleep in **BAGS** fixed to the wall. Otherwise we would float and bump around.

We **EXERCISE** a lot to keep fit and healthy.

There is no gravity in space so things need to be fixed down or they float around.

In space, there is no air. It changes from boiling hot to freezing cold in seconds. Tiny bits of space dust whizz around faster than a bullet. The space suit gives an astronaut air to breathe and protects against the cold, heat, and space dangers.

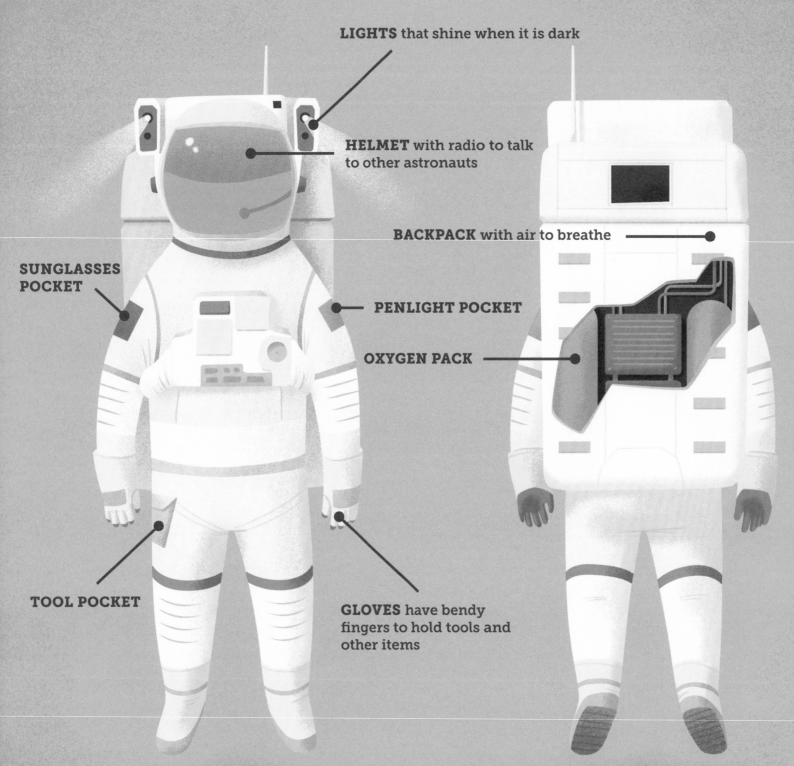

LIGHTS that shine when it is dark

HELMET with radio to talk to other astronauts

SUNGLASSES POCKET

PENLIGHT POCKET

BACKPACK with air to breathe

OXYGEN PACK

TOOL POCKET

GLOVES have bendy fingers to hold tools and other items

UNDERCLOTHES have tiny pipes to keep temperature comfortable

It takes an astronaut up to two hours to put on a space suit.

SPACE WALK

Going outside is called a "space walk" but it is more like a "space float." Astronauts walk in space to fix new gadgets and equipment. They make sure there is no damage and check experiments outside. The astronauts drift about, so a safety cord stops them from floating away into deep space. A long space walk can last eight hours or more. After a space walk, astronauts must rest and recover for many hours.

THE MOON

See me big and gleaming on dark nights.
I'm your Earth's closest friend. I call myself Moon.
Next time you look up, wave to me!

The **SURFACE** is dry and dusty with rocky hills and flat plains.

It is a quarter of the Earth's width.

More than 60 **MAN-MADE OBJECTS** are on the Moon, like rockets and moon buggies.

Long ago, many space rocks crashed into the Moon. They left wide bowl shapes called **CRATERS**.

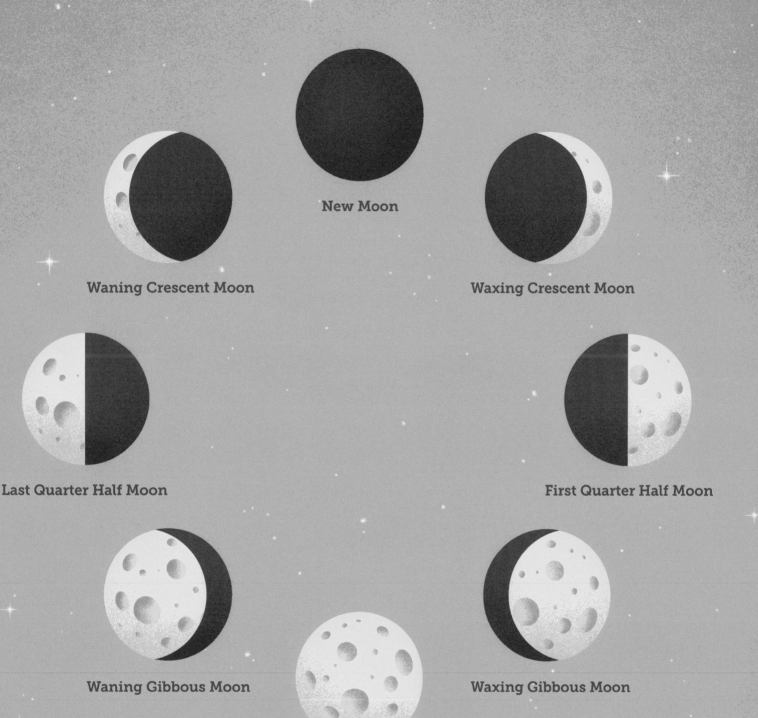

New Moon

Waning Crescent Moon

Waxing Crescent Moon

Last Quarter Half Moon

First Quarter Half Moon

Waning Gibbous Moon

Waxing Gibbous Moon

Full Moon

Some planets have many moons. Jupiter has nearly 70! Planet Earth has one moon. Because it is smaller than Earth it has less gravity. This means you would weigh six times less than on Earth and jump 10 times higher! It also seems to change shape, but it does not! It takes 28 days for our Moon to go around, or orbit, the Earth. We see a different view of the shiny part as it moves.

LANDING ON THE MOON

The quickest trip from Earth to the Moon and back took eight days.

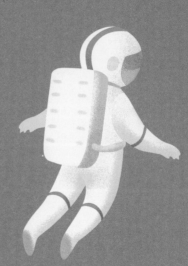

Some of the astronauts had an electric buggy called the **LUNAR ROVING VEHICLE**.

The astronauts collected **MOON SOIL AND ROCKS** to bring back to Earth.

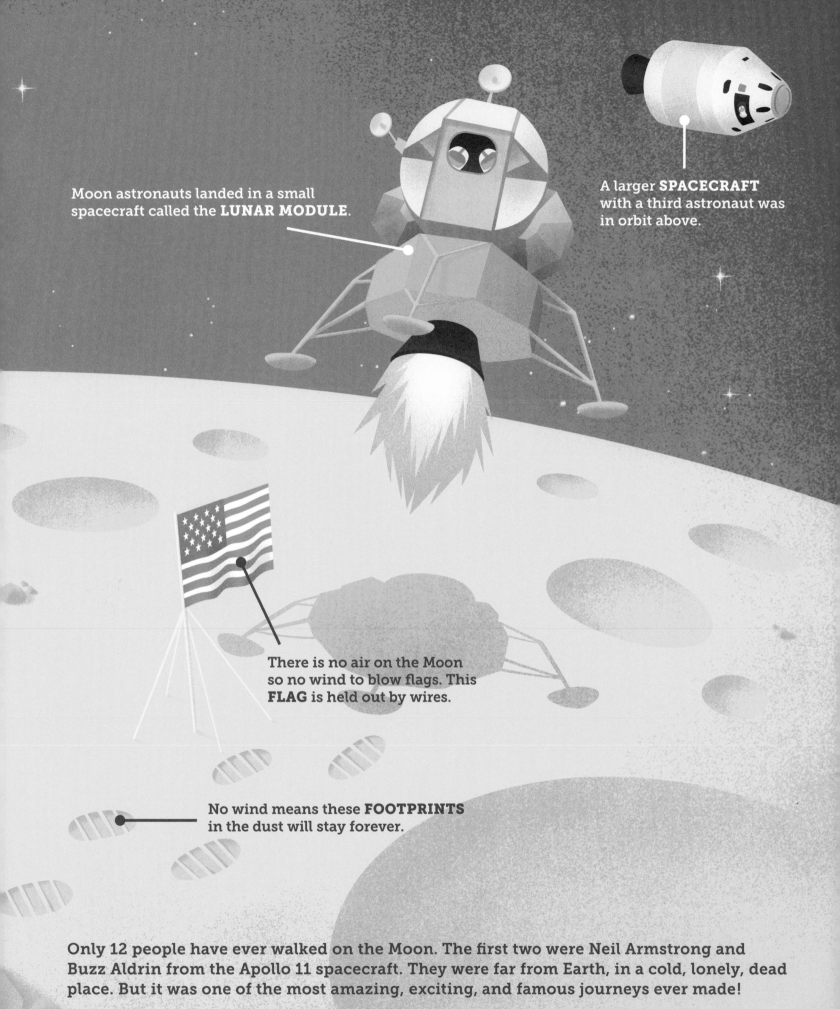

Moon astronauts landed in a small spacecraft called the **LUNAR MODULE**.

A larger **SPACECRAFT** with a third astronaut was in orbit above.

There is no air on the Moon so no wind to blow flags. This **FLAG** is held out by wires.

No wind means these **FOOTPRINTS** in the dust will stay forever.

Only 12 people have ever walked on the Moon. The first two were Neil Armstrong and Buzz Aldrin from the Apollo 11 spacecraft. They were far from Earth, in a cold, lonely, dead place. But it was one of the most amazing, exciting, and famous journeys ever made!

SPACE JUNK

We are left behind by people and that's the problem! We might smash into a satellite or crash into a spacecraft. We are Space Junk and no one wants us.

Some pieces are as small as your hand, like this ASTRONAUT'S LOST GLOVE.

Lots of space junk is going around the Earth right now. There are more than 30,000 pieces bigger than this book. Tidying away space junk will make space safer so people are planning a big space clean-up.

There are many OLD SATELLITES—one from 60 years ago!

Some bits of space junk are larger than trucks.

Bits of LEFTOVER ROCKETS litter much of space.

ANYONE OUT THERE?

I am <u>Life</u>. Life is a tree, or a whale, or you! But I can also be the tiniest, teeniest thing that grows, even a speck of slime!

So is there life in space? Scientists are on the hunt. For life to exist it needs water, light, and heat in exactly the right balance. Our planet Earth has it just right. Can we really be the only ones?

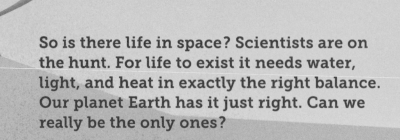

This is the **HUBBLE SPACE TELESCOPE**, which is as big as a school bus.

Some telescopes pick up **RADIO SIGNALS**.

Scientists try to find **CLUES** to life in the endless blackness. So far, nothing. But space is so BIG that they are sure there must be something, somewhere. There is still so much to discover ...

HUMAN HOME

Oceans, seas, lakes, and rivers! **WATER** is vital for life, and two-thirds of Earth's surface is water. Lucky for you, we're also the right distance from the Sun so it doesn't boil or freeze.

Above the surface is a mix of gases known as **AIR** or the **ATMOSPHERE**.

The Earth spins around once every 24 hours. When parts face the Sun we have day, and when they face away we have night. It takes one year for the Earth to make its journey around the Sun. On its journey, some parts are tilted towards the Sun and that makes summer. The parts tilted away have winter. This is how Earth's orbit continues to make seasons.

I am <u>planet Earth</u>, home to humans, plants, and animals. But I am the only place that is known to have life!

EARTH has been home to life for almost four billion years. That's most of the time the planet has existed. Today there are more than eight million different kinds of living things on Earth.

YOU

Look around you, little one.
The Earth is a wondrous place.
It is a place of animals, plants,
air, land, water ... and <u>you</u>!

Look up at me, high above and all around. A wondrous place of spinning galaxies, exploding stars, and planets teeming with the unknown.

Understand more about your world, and maybe one day you'll understand me too. I am Space. And you, my young explorer, are very special.

GLOSSARY

AIR The mixture of invisible gases floating around the surface of planet Earth. See also atmosphere.

ASTEROID A space rock that goes around the Sun but is too small to be a planet. Many asteroids have a lumpy, uneven shape, similar to potatoes, unlike ball-shaped planets.

ASTRONAUT A person who travels into space. Some animals that do so, like dogs and monkeys, are also called astronauts.

ATMOSPHERE The mixture of gases that surrounds a star and also some planets, moons, and other objects in space. Earth's atmosphere is often called air.

BIG BANG The event about 13.8 billion years ago, when a tiny speck of energy and matter exploded and began time, and space, and everything in it.

COMET A small space object, usually less then 6 miles across, that goes around the Sun on a very lopsided path.

CONSTELLATION A pattern of stars in the sky. Modern science names 88 constellations.

DEEP SPACE Space that is far, far from Earth, usually beyond our solar system.

EARTH The third of eight planets going around the Sun. It is made of rock, water and air. It is home to life, including us.

GALAXY A group of billions of stars fairly close together with vast empty space beyond.

GRAVITY A pulling force between every object and thing. The bigger and heavier the object, the stronger its gravity.

INTERNATIONAL SPACE STATION, ISS A large structure going around the Earth, with many rooms, machines, working places, and stores. Up to seven people live there at a time.

JETTISON To get rid of or fall off.

MILKY WAY The galaxy that contains our Sun and solar system.

MOON A natural space object that goes around a planet. Some moons are thousands of miles across.

MOON BUGGIES Small-wheeled electric vehicles that travel on the surface of a moon.

NEBULA A vast, wispy, hazy-looking cloud of gas. This is where stars form and die. Each nebula has a different size and shape.

ORBIT To go round and round another object in a curved path.

OXYGEN An invisible gas that forms about one-fifth of Earth's air or atmosphere, which all plants and animals need to stay alive.

PAYLOAD The objects carried by a craft or vehicle, such as satellites taken into space by a rocket.

PLANET A huge, ball-shaped object going around a star.

ROCKET A machine that travels very fast. It burns fuel to make a blast of gas to push it along.

SATELLITE An object that goes around or orbits another one. The Moon is a natural satellite of the Earth. But the word is usually used for man-made objects.

SEASONS The regular pattern of changing weather through the year. This is caused by the Earth's position as it goes around the Sun. Many places have four seasons: spring, summer, fall (autumn), and winter.

SOLAR PANELS Wide, flat parts that make electricity when sunlight shines on them.

SOLAR SYSTEM A star and all that goes around it, such as planets and their moons, asteroids and comets.

SPACE Everything anywhere away from planet Earth. Space starts 62 miles above the surface of our planet.

SPACE PROBE A robot-type spacecraft without people that travels a very long way into space.

SPACECRAFT A vehicle that travels into space. Some spacecrafts are no bigger than a suitcase and some are huge like the International Space Station.

STAR A massive ball-shaped object in space that gives out light, heat, and other forms of energy.

SUN The Sun is our nearest star, about 93 million miles away. Its light and heat power life on Earth.

TELESCOPE A device that makes far away things seem nearer and bigger.

TEMPERATURE A measure of how hot or cold something is. Temperature is in degrees Celsius (°C) or Fahrenheit (°F).

VOLCANO A gap in the surface of the Earth that spurts red-hot flowing rocks, burning gases, and ash clouds. There are also volcanoes on some other planets and moons.

WATER A liquid with no color or smell. It is is needed for life on Earth.

SPACE KIDS

An Introduction
for Young Explorers

Illustrated by **ANDREA DE SANTIS**
Written by **STEVE PARKER**

The book was conceived, edited and designed
by **GESTALTEN**.

Edited by **ANGELA FRANCIS** and
ROBERT KLANTEN
Design and layout by **BRITTA VAN KESTEREN** and
MONA OSTERKAMP

Typefaces: Forgotten Futurist by **RAY LARABIE**,
and Museo Slab by **JOS BUIVENGA**

Printed by **NINO DRUCK GMBH**,
Neustadt/Weinstr.
Made in Germany

Published by Little Gestalten, Berlin 2018
ISBN 978-3-89955-795-4

The German edition is also available under
ISBN 978-3-89955-794-7

For more information, and to order books, please visit
little.gestalten.com.

Bibliographic information published by the Deutsche
Nationalbibliothek: The Deutsche Nationalbibliothek
lists this publication in the Deutsche National-
bibliografie; detailed bibliographic data are available
online at http://dnb.d-nb.de.

This book was printed on paper certified according to
the standards of the FSC®.